WORLDfocus
Kenya

DAVID MARSHALL
GEOFF SAYER

Contents

Introduction

Tropic of Cancer

Equator

Tropic of Capricorn

You may have watched television programmes about the wildlife in Kenya, or talked to people who have been on holiday there. If you have, then you may think of Kenya as a country of palm-fringed beaches, snow-topped mountains and exciting wild animals like lions and leopards, elephants and rhinos, giraffe and wildebeest.

You may have heard of Kenya's capital, Nairobi. It is a busy modern city with shops and hotels, factories and skyscrapers, a university and parliament buildings. If you were only to visit Nairobi, or the beaches and wildlife parks, you would not really know Kenya at all.

Kenya is about the same size as France. It lies in East Africa, with a coastline on the Indian Ocean. A striking feature of the landscape is the Rift Valley which runs for 4000 kilometres through Africa. In Kenya there are highlands on both sides of the Rift Valley, rising to the icy summit of Mount Kenya. At 5199 metres it is Africa's second highest mountain.

△ **Where is Kenya?**

▽ **Looking across the Rift Valley near Nairobi.**

The Rift Valley has been called the 'Cradle of Mankind'. Here, scientists have found the skeletons and stone tools of early humans. Some of the finds are over 2 million years old. The first human beings may have developed in this part of Africa.

Kenya lies on the Equator, so the sun rises at about 7 a.m. and sets at about 7 p.m. every day of the year. Kenyans do not talk of winter and summer; they talk instead about wet and dry seasons. In most of the country the drier months are between June and September.

 Map of Kenya showing relief and main geographical features.

Close to the coast it is hot and humid, with rain during most of the year. There is good rainfall in the southwest, in the highlands and around Lake Victoria, too. This area provides much of Kenya's agricultural land.

The highlands are over 1500 metres above sea-level. At this level the climate is **temperate**. It is warm but not hot.

The lands to the north and east, which make up over two-thirds of the country, are hotter and drier. Much of this is 'bush' country, where people live mainly by keeping cows, goats, sheep and camels.

The people

Today's Kenya is a rich mixture of lifestyles and languages. For over a thousand years East Africa has been a meeting point for different peoples and different ways of life. Groups of farmers and **herders** moved onto the land from the south and the north. Each group brought its own **culture** with its own dress and building style, its own music and art, language and beliefs.

Some settled on the coast looking out onto a wider world. Traders crossing the Indian Ocean brought goods from Arabia, Persia, India and Indonesia. In this way bananas first came to East Africa, where they are now widely grown. Small sailing boats called **dhows** came to Mombasa, Malindi and other ports to buy and sell gold, ivory, cloth, glass and tools.

Arab influence was strong, and the people on the coast developed a distinct way of life. They became known as the Swahili, an Arabic word meaning 'coast-dwellers'. Their language, Kiswahili, was mainly African with a mixture of Arabic. Today it is the national language of Kenya and its neighbour, Tanzania.

△ Many people settled along Kenya's coast. This is the waterfront at Lamu.

The Islamic religion also spread along the coast, where it remains strong. **Missionaries** from European churches travelled inland bringing Christianity. In modern Kenya over half the people are Christians.

In the last hundred years life has changed very quickly for the people of East Africa. Before 1895 there was no country called Kenya. People organized themselves within their own groups, or clans. On the coast there were town governments.

This changed between 1870 and 1914, when European countries invaded Africa. Britain sent its soldiers and took over much of East Africa. They created the colony of Kenya, which was ruled from London. The best land was taken from the Africans by settlers from Britain and became known as the White Highlands. A chief described how this news came to his people: 'A Pink Cheek came and told us of his King who lived over the seas. "This great king is now your king," he said, "and this land is all his land." This was strange news, for the land was ours...'.

Kenya finally became an **independent** country in 1963. Jomo Kenyatta led the struggle against British rule and became the first President of the Republic of Kenya.

British rule has left its mark on Kenya. English is widely spoken, and systems of law and government are based on the English way.

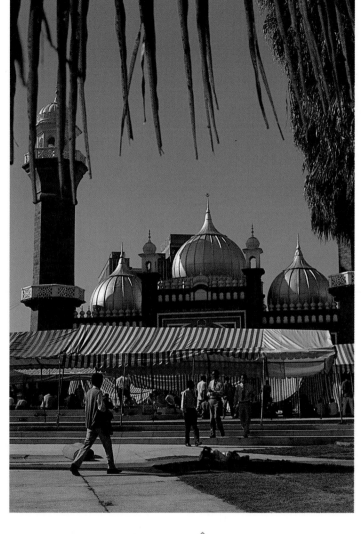

△ The Jamia mosque in Nairobi where Muslims go to pray.

Where do people live?

Kenya has a population of about 25 million. On average there are 43 people for each square kilometre, compared with about 230 in the same area in the UK. Almost all Kenya's population is African. There are about 200,000 Kenyans of European, Asian or Arabic origin.

Kenya's capital, Nairobi, has a population of almost 1.5 million. Other major cities include Kisumu, Nakuru and the port of Mombasa. A quarter of the population lives in the rapidly growing towns.

If you were to travel around Kenya you would see many different ways of life. You might see Gabbra people lead their camel trains across the dry northern plains, as they have for centuries. A group of Kamba women sing as they work together, turning over the soil in a maize field with their hoes. A Kikuyu trader piles up cooking pots and brightly-coloured plastic bowls on her market stall. Luo children pound cassava roots into flour on a rock beside Lake Victoria. An Asian shopkeeper rearranges the video-recorders in his city store to catch the eye of passing customers. A Somali herder milks her goats, calling them out of their pen by name: 'Ouley, Bariar, Hale, Jogbela...'

△ Wangoi in Uhuru Park, Nairobi.

Many people have moved from the country to the towns to try to make a better living. Sometimes men come alone looking for work, hoping to send money back to their families. People find jobs in shops, offices and factories. Others may work as nannies, cleaners and night-watchmen in the wealthy suburbs, or sell newspapers, soft drinks, sweets and peanuts in the city.

Wangoi is ten years old. She came to Nairobi with her mother and brother. They left their small farm when her father died. They live in Kibera, an area of poor housing.

Wangoi describes their life in Nairobi: 'Most days I walk into town with my mother, to see what's happening – she's selling peanuts in the park. My brother Mwangi is here too. We don't like Nairobi. We want to go back to Murang'a, to go to school. Mother will take us back when she has enough money – she says, when she's saved enough.'

Life can be difficult in the city.

Agriculture

Most people in Kenya are farmers. In the fertile highlands, farms are usually **smallholdings** of less than one hectare; about the size of a soccer pitch.

Many families grow enough maize, bananas, beans, potatoes and other vegetables to provide food for the whole year. They may have one or two cows for milk, and a few chickens. This is known as **subsistence** farming: they produce enough to feed themselves.

People need money, too, to buy clothes, shoes, tools and fertilizers, and to pay for medicine and school books. They sell some of their food crops, perhaps at the town market. They can also grow and sell **cash crops** such as coffee, tea, sugar and cotton. More than half of the coffee and tea produced in Kenya is grown by smallholders.

▽ Maize and beans growing on small farms in the highlands.

There are large farms in Kenya as well, rearing cattle and growing tea, coffee and wheat. The company *Brooke Bond* owns huge plantations of tea bushes around Kericho. The green leaves are plucked and dried in nearby factories, producing much of the tea that is sold in British shops.

Most of the tea and coffee which Kenya grows is **exported**, which means it is sold and shipped to other countries. These two crops make up almost half of the money which Kenya earns from its exports. Kenya has to earn this money in order to pay for the things it buys in from other countries. Some farmers are growing new export crops, such as French beans and chillies, strawberries and mangoes, and flowers.

On the drier lands which make up most of Kenya, people live differently. In the driest, or **arid**, areas they keep **livestock** such as cows, sheep, goats and camels. Families live off the milk, meat and skins of their animals. These can also be sold at the market. Where there is a little more rainfall, farmers plant fast-growing cereal crops like millet and sorghum.

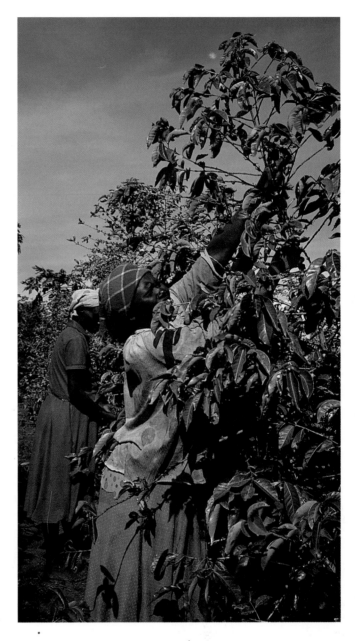

△ These women are picking coffee beans.

Women do much of the work in a farming family, both in the home and on the land. On small farms the land is cultivated by hand, with the use of a tool called a hoe. Wealthier farmers may use a plough, pulled by oxen or a tractor.

Industry

Kenya's industries are the most developed in East Africa. They sell products inside Kenya, and export some to neighbouring countries like Uganda and Tanzania. In shops and markets you can see names well known in Britain, such as *Colgate* toothpaste, *Dulux* paint, *Lux* soap, *EverReady* batteries and *Johnson's* baby powder. These are not **imports** bought in from other countries; they are made in Kenya.

Most of Kenya's large industries were set up to process farm products. Maize is milled to produce flour, known as 'unga'. This is used in almost every home to cook ugali, a stiff porridge. Wheat flour is used to make bread and cakes in the town bakeries. Cotton is spun and woven to produce cloth. Other factories refine sugar from sugar-cane, process milk and beef, use barley to brew beer and tobacco to make cigarettes.

Kenya has little coal, gas or oil of its own. Much of the money which the country earns from its exports is spent on buying oil. Kenya also imports all of its iron and steel, and most of the machinery used in its factories.

Many people make and sell things to earn a living. They become metal-workers, tailors, shoemakers, carpenters, flower-sellers or market traders. This is known as 'Jua Kali', which means 'hot sun', because they usually have to work outside in the hot sun!

Metal goods being made at Kamukunji Jua Kali.

Tourists visit Amboseli Park to see the wildlife.

The ceaseless clatter of hammers and chisels on metal echoes through Kamukunji Jua Kali in Nairobi. Behind stalls crammed with shining goods, men are busy turning old oil drums and other scrap into lamps, cooking stoves, water heaters, buckets, bed-frames, jugs and cooking pots. There are few tools and no workbenches, just the dusty ground.

Tourism is another important source of **income** for Kenya, and provides jobs for over 100,000 Kenyans. Every year half a million visitors come to spend their money at the beaches and wildlife parks. However, tourism has made life difficult for some Kenyans. Herders like the Maasai and Samburu have been thrown off the land where they used to live, to make space for the parks. But they receive very little of the money which the tourists spend.

Kenya's challenge

Kenya does not have a large population for its size. But there is a shortage of good agricultural land. In a year of normal rainfall, Kenya can grow enough food for its people. In years of poor rainfall, like 1992-93, food has to be imported. Some of this food is sent by other countries as **food aid**.

△ Villagers giving out wheat and oil as food aid.

It is poor Kenyans who are most likely to go without food, who live in broken-down housing, who miss out on schooling and health-care. Their **poverty** is not simply an accident. Like most African countries, Kenya is changing rapidly. These changes can make some groups of people more **vulnerable**, more likely to be pushed into poverty.

If families have land they can produce their own food. In Kenya land is not shared equally. White farmers took most of the best land when Kenya was ruled by Britain. When the country became independent many of these farms were divided among smallholders. But almost half remain as large farms, owned by less than 4000 wealthy Kenyan farmers.

The Maasai and Samburu peoples live by herding livestock. But much of their best land is being taken for wildlife parks and for agriculture. This destroys their way of life, which depends on sharing vast areas of dry grazing land. The herders become less able to cope with drought, the periods of low rainfall which come every few years.

If you are a Kenyan woman you are also much more likely to become poor. Women do more work than men but are less likely to have money, go to school or take part in making decisions.

Disagreements which lead to fighting also bring poverty. Kenya has been a peaceful country. But since 1991 thousands of Kenyans have been driven from their homes by fighting in western Kenya. These clashes are linked to the shortage of agricultural land. But they have also been influenced by changes which have introduced a **multi-party** political system in Kenya, like the one we have in Britain. Elections have caused tension between different groups in Kenya.

Kenyans will work to produce more food, to sell more goods to other countries and to earn more from tourism. The challenge for the country is to achieve this without pushing more people to the edge of poverty. Above all, people everywhere in Kenya need to have a real say in the decisions that affect them and their way of life.

△ **Women have the task of collecting water for the home.**

Iltilal – A Maasai village

Iltilal is a village in southern Kenya, close to the border with Tanzania. It lies on a flat, grassy plain close to Tsavo National Park. Tsavo is the largest wildlife park in Kenya.

Most of the people in Iltilal are Maasai. They are **pastoralists.** They make a living from their cows, goats and sheep. There are many Maasai villages like Iltilal in Kenya and Tanzania, the neighbouring country.

Most of the land around Iltilal is too dry to grow crops, but livestock can survive by moving from place to place in search of grass and shrubs. There are no fences. People make arrangements to share all the land.

In the dry season, between June and September, the land becomes bare and dusty. Only the thorny, wide-spreading acacia trees stay green, providing welcome shade in the middle of the day. At this time of year the cows have to be taken far from Iltilal to look for better grazing.

△ Iltilal during the rainy season.

The rains that come between October and May quickly make the land turn green. Livestock can feed close to the home, and milk is plentiful. Cattle can be sold, and are killed and eaten on special occasions. But milk is the most important food in Iltilal.

There are about 200 homesteads in the village. A homestead is made up of several families who live together, each with their own house. They share the job of looking after the cows.

Inside each homestead the houses are dotted in a rough circle around the main **boma** or cattle enclosure. The boma is fenced with branches cut from thorn trees. At night this protects the cows against thieves, and predators such as lions.

Most houses are made from materials found in Iltilal. Walls and rafters are made from wooden poles tied together with string made from tree bark. The domed roof is covered with grass and the walls with mud and cow dung. There is no window. A single doorway winds into the house at an angle, like the entrance to a giant snail shell.

A dusty, dirt road links Iltilal to the nearest town, Loitokitok, 60 kilometres away. In the other direction the road leads into Tsavo Park. At the roadside in the village there is a small shop and a tea-room, built with sheets of corrugated iron. Nearby is a Health Centre, with a water pump used by the villagers. A little further from the main road are the primary school and the church.

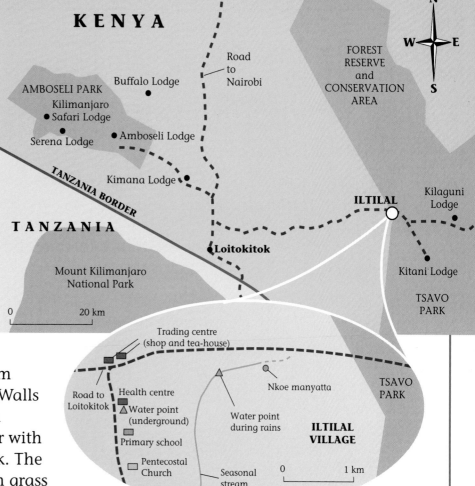

The village of Iltilal.

▷ **Taking cattle out of the homestead early in the morning.**

Life in Iltilal

Women do most of the work around the homestead. It is a woman's job to build the house, milk the animals and provide food and water for the family.

Children of about five years and older are expected to help. They care for younger children, collect water, wash dishes and look after the calves. As they become older, girls work around the homestead with their mothers. Boys and young men take the cattle out to graze.

Older men make decisions that affect each homestead. They meet to discuss matters which affect the whole community of Iltilal. The local chief, Nkonina Songoi, was chosen as a leader when he was young. People respect his ideas.

▽ **Families leaving Iltilal church after the Christmas service.**

But things are changing in Iltilal. Elders must deal with government officials, who may have different ideas from them. The primary school has made a big difference to the lives of the children. At school they learn about Kenya and its history. They also learn English and Kiswahili, the national language.

The nurse at the Health Centre has brought modern medical care to the village. Many of the girls at school now say they want to become nurses, too. The nearby town, Loitokitok, has grown rapidly. People in Iltilal can now sell and buy things more easily.

There are other changes which are more difficult for the villagers to cope with. In the dry season the cattle were taken to better grazing land, where there was more rain. This land was kept especially for this purpose. Tsavo Park used to be dry season grazing land. But the Maasai are no longer allowed to take cattle there in case they disturb the wild animals – and the tourists! Other important grazing areas have been taken by farmers to grow crops.

The Maasai do not kill wild animals for meat. Zebra, giraffe and antelope still roam across their land. They did not choose to have the game parks. Now there are new ideas about dividing and fencing the people's land. But who will make the decisions? Will it be business people in Loitokitok, or the government in Nairobi? Or will the people of Iltilal be allowed to make their own choices?

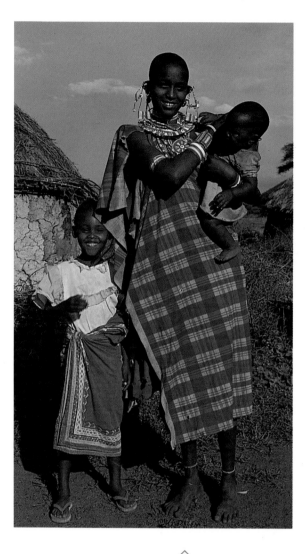

△ Women like Nonkipa do most of the work around the homestead. Here she is with her baby and her niece Tido.

Education

The number of schools has grown rapidly since Kenya became an independent country in 1963. Children start school when they are about six years old. Most spend eight years at primary school, passing from Standard One to Standard Eight.

Some children drop out of school because their parents need their help at home. This happens most in country areas like Iltilal, where schools have only been built in recent years. In the past, children had their schooling at home, learning the skills needed to look after cattle or grow crops.

Now things are changing. Nice Nkoe is fifteen years old. She is the first girl to stay on to Standard Eight at Iltilal School, but many more will follow. Her cousin Consolata who is twelve, in Standard Five, is likely to be one. 'I'd hate anyone who tried to stop me going to school,' she said. 'I miss it in the holidays.'

Nice usually walks to school with her cousins and her sister, Mankushai, who is ten. They leave home at about 7.30 a.m. to reach school in time for the start of lessons at 8 a.m. They finish at 3.45 p.m., with an hour's break for lunch. All the children wear school uniforms.

Nice and her cousin, Kilesi, are just finishing Standard Eight. They have taken the important final exams which all children complete in the last year of primary school.

Nice enjoys school. 'My favourite subject is English – today we read *A Visit to Turkana*. It's interesting because none of us have ever been there. The Turkana people keep cows, but they're very different from the Maasai!'

New classrooms being built at Iltilal School.

Nice and Kilesi setting off for school.

'We spend most time on science and GHC (Geography, History and Civics). We learn a lot about Kenya. Then there's maths, Kiswahili and religious education. We don't do much sport – the teachers say it's too hot. They aren't from Maasailand!'

Nice has plans for her future. 'I want to be a doctor or a nurse, so I can work in Loitokitok hospital and help the people who live in this area. First I have to get to secondary school. I'll need high marks in my exams to get there.'

Children spend four years in secondary school. There are only places for one in five children, and parents have to pay part of the cost.

△ Nice and Hamisi share a book during their English lesson.

Spare time

In Iltilal the younger children play games that are found almost everywhere in the world. They might start playing tig as they look after the calves, or draw lines in the earth to see who can jump the furthest.

Consolata describes other popular games: 'We make houses. We can use sticks and grass, or just stones to mark the walls. Someone acts as mother, someone as father, others as the children. We play ball games like kati. We stand in a circle and try to hit the person in the middle.'

Days are spent outside, because the climate is warm. The children have lots of space and lots of freedom. They do not have to be warned about talking to strangers, or being careful about how they cross the road. They just have to watch out for snakes, and possibly even lions!

△ Consolata leads a dancing game. She is facing you.

◁ A women's group singing at the harambee.

▷ Bao is a popular game in Kenya.

Nice and Consolata both sing in the school choir. In her last month at primary school, Nice led the choir at a harambee. This was a local show to raise money for the school. A total of 64,000 shillings (over £1000) was collected! 'Harambee' means people joining together to help themselves.

At school, children like to play football, netball and volleyball. Kenyans are great runners, too. In the 1992 Olympics Kenya won gold medals in the men's 800, 1500, 3000 and 5000 metre races.

As they grow up, most Kenyan children have a different idea of play to children in Europe. Work and play are not separate. 'We enjoy ourselves when we go out together to collect wood or water,' Nice explained. 'It's not hard work.'

An important reason for this big difference is that Kenyan children are usually part of a close-knit family. They think more of doing things for their families than doing things for themselves. Jobs are usually shared with brothers, sisters, cousins or friends, giving the children a chance to chat and joke together. There are always aunts, uncles and grandparents to turn to for advice.

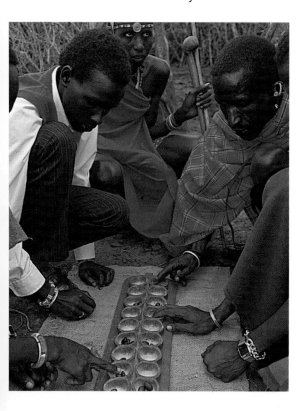

In the large towns life is different. For those who have money there are cinemas and restaurants, swimming pools and sports centres, fairgrounds and video games. But family relationships can become less important to people when they go to live in a town.

A day with the Nkoe family

Thorn fencing

Gate

Gate

Thorn fencing

Gate

Main Cattle Enclosure (BOMA)

0   20 m

N
E
W
S

Gate

⑤
④
③
①
②
Ⓓ
Ⓒ
Ⓔ
Ⓐ
Ⓑ

Gate

Gate

Gate

Ⓐ Jackson and Lucy
Ⓑ Consolata
Ⓒ Kilesi
Ⓓ Grandma Njieroo
Ⓔ Nice, her sister
    Mankushai,
    aunt Mary and
    cousin Tido

Thorn fencing

1-5 Pens for calves
▪ Warriors' house
▪ Traditional Maasai homes
▪ Timber home with iron roof
▪ Mud-walled home with iron roof
▪ Toilet
▪ Shed

◁ Where people live in the Nkoe manyatta, Iltilal.

▷ Lucy and Mary cooking ugali and potatoes in the kitchen.

Work in the homestead begins before sunrise. The women are up first, moving quietly through the grey half-light. A smell of smoke hangs in the still air as fires are lit in the kitchens. Cows begin to stir in the boma.

Nice gets washed and dressed. Usually she would be getting ready for school. But it is late November, and the schools have closed for the long holiday.

Nice greets her mother, Lucy, and aunt Mary. She then goes out to collect water with her younger sister, Mankushai, and her cousins, Tido and Consolata. After recent good rainfall, they can fill their containers from the small stream close to the homestead.

Nice's cousin, Kilesi, is also up early. He helps to open the cattle-gates and take the cows out of the homestead. Nice comes back to join the women who are milking the cows in the early morning sunshine. There are over 200 cows, but each woman knows which are hers.

▽ Lucy and Jackson outside their timber bungalow.

In the kitchen Nice's grandmother, Njieroo, and Tido drink mugs of milk, still warm from the cows. Milk and sugar are boiled to make tea. Nice takes a mug to her father, Jackson. For those who want it there's ugali from the previous evening. Ugali is boiled maize-meal broken off and eaten with the fingers, like bread.

Kilesi and his brothers take the cattle towards the Chyulu Hills to find the best grazing. The younger boys and girls take the calves to graze close to the homestead.

The homestead is quiet in the heat of the day. Jackson talks with his brothers and other elders. He is employed by the government to watch out for poachers around Tsavo Park.

Nice washes clothes, helped by Tido. As the day cools, Nice and her aunt Mary go to collect more water. The

calves are brought back to their pens, and as the sun sets the young herders return with the cattle. Nice comes to milk her family's cows again, this time inside the homestead. The light fades quickly. As the mosquitoes start to bite, people move indoors and sit around the fire.

Jackson lights an oil lamp. The men are fed first, and eat separately. The women and children eat in the kitchen by the light of the cooking fire. The day ends as it started – with the sounds of the women working, cleaning the plates and pots.

Travel around Iltilal

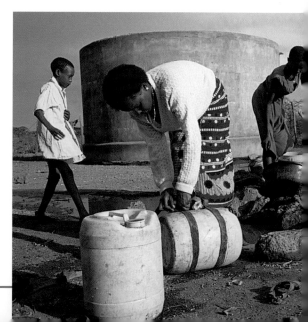

Nice and Lucy at the market in Loitokitok.

Nice collects water in Iltilal and walks home. The concrete tank is filled with water pumped from underground.

Pastoralists like the Maasai are very good walkers. They think nothing of walking 40 kilometres in a day to tend cattle or visit relatives.

In Iltilal, most of the things people need are within walking distance. They walk to the water pump, to the shop, to the woods, to school, to the Health Centre and the church. Donkeys are used as 'burden' animals, to carry water, firewood and other goods. They are essential when families move their homes.

People in Iltilal do not own cars. But the world of rapid travel, of aeroplanes and cars, does reach into Iltilal. Every week dozens of mini-vans hurry through the village, bringing tourists from Europe and America to Tsavo Park. They rarely stop to talk to the villagers. 'They come and they leave knowing nothing about us,' says Chief Songoi. Travel does not always broaden the mind.

Loitokitok is the nearest town to Iltilal. People go there to buy the things they cannot easily get in the village, such as maize-meal and tea, sugar and salt, clothes and shoes, cooking pots, bowls and mugs. Nice and her mother travel to town about once a month, when they can get a lift with a lorry or van.

At first the rough, dirt road to Loitokitok passes through grassland similar to Iltilal. There are few vehicles apart from tourist vans. As the road climbs gently towards Loitokitok the landscape changes. Groups of women are sowing maize and beans in ploughed fields. There is better rainfall here. This used to be pastoralist land, kept for grazing cows in the dry season. Now farmers have bought it and fenced it off.

▽ Tourist mini-vans travelling in convoy towards Tsavo Park from Loitokitok.

Loitokitok lies on the lower slope of Kilimanjaro, Africa's highest mountain. After heavy overnight rain, young men push wooden barrows through the mud. They are paid to carry goods to the market. Small mini-buses arrive at the market entrance, their roofs piled high with boxes and bags of vegetables and fruit. In the market, produce is set out on sacks. You might see beans, carrots, peas, cabbages, tomatoes, potatoes, oranges, mangos and bananas. Most of the buyers and sellers are women.

Nice buys a dress from one of the shops. Lucy buys some vegetables and maize-meal. By the time they leave, the town has fallen under the shadow of the great mountain.

Travel around Kenya

Most travel in Kenya is done on foot, especially in country areas. Turkana women like Arukudi Lobe will travel more than 100 kilometres to collect wild fruits. 'We walk for two or three days, beyond these hills as far as Kokuro before returning on the fourth day. We carry home soft fruits like Emeyen, Ekalale, Edome, Elero and Eng'omo. And Edung and Edapal, which have to be boiled with fire ash.'

Pastoralists often pack up their homesteads and move with their livestock. Then they use donkeys or camels to carry young children and the mats and poles from which they build their homes.

Bikes are used widely too, although it is often frowned on for women to ride them, except as passengers sitting side-saddle on the crossbar. Around Lake Victoria men ride home with huge fish called Nile Perch draped across their bikes. Sometimes a bike may be so heavily loaded that it has to be pushed, not ridden. It might be carrying 100 kilograms of cotton or bananas.

△ **Kenyatta Avenue in Nairobi. The word 'uhuru' on the banner means 'freedom'.**

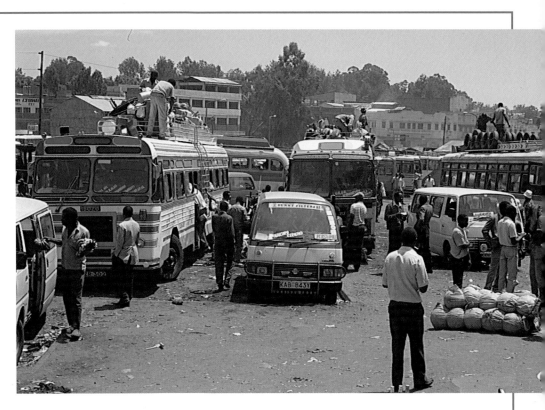

Machakos Bus Station in Nairobi.

Buses are used by most people to get around town. The brightly-painted coaches are called matatus or manyangas. Kenyans crowding on to the packed coaches to get to and from work will sometimes wait for their favourite manyanga, perhaps one with a careful driver, or the softest seats and best music system.

Buses are the most popular way of moving around the country. Those who want to travel out of Nairobi go to 'Machakos Airport', the name jokingly given to the city's busy Machakos Bus Station. This is the noisy, colourful starting point for long journeys up-country, as Kenyans working in the city go back home to see relatives and friends.

Less than one out of every hundred people in Kenya owns a car, but cities like Nairobi, Mombasa and Nakuru still have traffic jams.

Kenya's main railway line links the port of Mombasa to Kisumu and Kampala, the capital of Uganda. The railway was built by the British between 1896 and 1904 to open up trade. It seems incredible that Kenya's modern capital, Nairobi, began its life then as a railway camp.

Images of Kenya

Everywhere you travel in Kenya, you can find Kenyans working to meet the challenges that face the country.

If you visited Machakos you might hear Kyungu women's group singing while they work together to improve their fields. They have built terraces which are earth banks that stretch across the hillsides. The terraces trap the rain and stop it from washing the soil downhill. 'When we plant maize, beans and onions, they are bigger in size now,' explains Munjira Maleve. There are thousands of groups like Kyungu, and they have terraced most of the land in Machakos.

△ A meeting of disabled people in Wajir. Asia Mude is closest to the camera.

In Wajir town, you would be welcomed and asked to sit in the sunshine and talk with disabled people who have formed an Association. 'As a disabled person on my own, I couldn't do anything,' explains Asia Mude. 'But when lots of us get together, we can press the government to provide proper services.' Geddo Ali, who like Asia is blind, is about to begin teaching at Wajir Secondary School. 'I'm going to encourage parents to send disabled children to the school. I want to show them that they can manage on their own – like me!'

In Busia in western Kenya you might meet Margaret Afandi riding her bike to call on her neighbours. Margaret and her husband grow all their family's food on just a half-hectare of land. They also have more than 100 chickens' eggs to sell each day. Margaret is an **organic** farmer. She uses manure and compost on her land, rather than expensive fertilizers. Now she spends time visiting neighbours to pass on her ideas.

▷ A women's group collecting stones to build a shop.

And back again in Wajir, ten-year-old Ibrahim Sheikh might come over to talk to you, as he did to me. His family lost all their camels and goats and have come to live close to the town. They cannot afford to pay anything towards Ibrahim's schooling. 'But I'm top of the class!' Ibrahim tells me proudly.

Thinking perhaps that I don't believe him, he runs off towards his home about 3 kilometres away. Less than an hour later he comes panting back with a sheet of paper which he carefully unfolds. 'See, "Position in class: 1",' he laughs.

If Kenya can provide schooling for all its children, it will be better able to meet the challenges of the future.

Glossary

Arid Dry, having little rain. In Kenya areas which receive less than 200 mm of rain each year are officially described as arid.

Cash crops Crops which are grown to be sold rather than eaten by the farmers themselves. This can include food crops, such as vegetables or maize, which can be taken to a nearby town market or sold to traders. Coffee and tea are important cash crops which are grown mainly for selling to other countries.

Culture A people's whole way of life. This includes their ideas, beliefs, language, values, knowledge, customs and the things they make.

Exports Goods sold and transported to other countries.

Food aid Foodstuff given to those who are unable to provide for themselves. Food aid is usually given by one country to another, either directly or through the United Nations World Food Programme. Maize and wheat are most commonly used for food aid.

Herder Someone who looks after a herd of animals, such as cows, camels, sheep or goats.

Hydroelectric station A place where machinery produces electricity from flowing water. In Kenya rivers are dammed to produce a strong flow of water. In some countries the ebb and flow of sea tides is used to make electricity.

Imports Goods brought in from other countries.

Income Money received. Tourism, and the sale of exports such as tea and coffee, bring money into Kenya. This provides income for Kenyan workers and for the government.

Independent Not depending on others. Free to act or make decisions. A country is said to be independent when it is free to govern itself, and is not ruled by another country.

Livestock Animals such as cows, goats, camels, sheep and pigs kept by farmers or herders.

Matatu Small private bus or mini-van. The word comes from 'tatu', which in Kiswahili means 'three', because the original fare in Nairobi was three cents. Bigger, brightly painted coaches with soft seats and loud music systems are call 'manyangas'.

Missionaries People who are sent by their church to do religious work in a foreign country. Early missionaries brought Christianity to Africans.

Multi-party A political system which allows more than one political party. Until 1991 Kenya was a One-Party State, ruled by the Kenya African National Union (KANU). The first multi-party election was held in 1992.

Organic farmer A farmer who grows crops using fertilizers and pest-killers made from or by plants and animals. For example, animal manure and compost made from rotted plants are used as fertilizers. In this way the farmer avoids the dangers of artificial chemical products, and saves money.

Pastoralists People who mainly depend on livestock to make their living. They use the milk, meat and blood of their animals for food. Other animal products, such as skins, are sold or used to make clothes, houses, tools and containers. Pastoralists are often nomadic, travelling long distances to find fresh grazing for their animals.

Poverty The condition of being poor. People can be reduced to poverty if their way of life is threatened, or if they do not have enough land, money or other resources to enjoy a reasonable standard of life. Poverty differs from one country to another. People in Britain feel they are poor if they do not own a car or a TV. Only wealthy people in Kenya would hope to own such things.

Temperate Moderate, not extreme. A temperate climate is one which is neither very hot nor very cold.

Vulnerable Unprotected, easily hurt or damaged. If farmers, for example, cannot save enough money or good crops from their harvests, they become vulnerable. Poor rainfall and one bad harvest may push them into poverty.

Index

About Oxfam in Kenya

Oxfam works with poor people and their organizations in over 80 countries. Oxfam believes that all people have basic rights: to earn a living, and to have food, shelter, health care and education. Oxfam provides relief in emergencies, and gives long-term support to people struggling to build a better life for themselves and their families.

Oxfam's established programme in Kenya actively encourages poor people to consider the causes of their poverty and to take action to improve their circumstances. This requires investment in people, to inspire confidence and give practical and organizational skills. Oxfam uses this approach in its four main areas of work in Kenya. Oxfam works with women, ensuring they are involved in all projects. Work is done with nomadic people, or pastoralists, and community-based health care is promoted. Finally, Oxfam works with farmers in areas with poor soil and unreliable rainfall, to help them produce enough food for their families.

The publishers would like to thank the following for their help in preparing this book: Geoff Sayer from Oxfam who took on the role of co author at very short notice; Ian Leggell and the staff of the Oxfam East Africa Desk; the people of Iltilal; the staff at the Oxfam Nairobi office; the staff of the Oxfam photo library; and the Oxfam Education workers who commented on early drafts.

The Oxfam Education Catalogue lists a range of other resources on economically developing countries, including Kenya, and issues of development. These materials are produced by Oxfam, by other agencies, and by Development Education Centres. For a copy of the catalogue contact Oxfam, 274 Banbury Road, Oxford OX2 7DZ, phone (0865) 311311, or your national Oxfam office.

Photographic acknowledgements
The authors and publishers wish to acknowledge, with thanks, the following photographic sources:

Geoff Sayer/Oxfam pp 2, 3, 5, 8, 10-29; Peter Barker/Panos Pictures p4; J. Spafford/Oxfam p9; Karen Twining/Oxfam p29.

The publishers have made every effort to trace the copyright holders, but if they have inadvertently overlooked any, they will be pleased to make the necessary arrangement at the first opportunity.

Cover photograph © Oxfam/Geoff Sayer – Turkana children in northern Kenya.

Note to the reader - In this book there are some words in the text which are printed in **bold** type. This shows that the word is listed in the glossary on page 30. The glossary gives a brief explanation of words which may be new to you.

First published in Great Britain by Heinemann Library an imprint of Heinemann Educational Publishers Halley Court, Jordan Hill, Oxford OX2 8EJ a division of Reed Educational & Professional Publishing Ltd

MELBOURNE AUCKLAND
FLORENCE PRAGUE MADRID ATHENS
SINGAPORE TOKYO SAO PAULO
CHICAGO PORTSMOUTH (NH) MEXICO
IBADAN GABORONE JOHANNESBURG
KAMPALA NAIROBI

© 1994 Heinemann Library

98 97 96
10 9 8 7 6 5 4 3 2

British Library Cataloguing in Publication Data is available from the British Library on request.

ISBN 0 431 07252 3 (Hardback)

ISBN 0 431 07255 8 (Paperback)

Designed and produced by Visual Image
Cover design by Threefold Design

Printed in China